RETRANSITION

Kate Goodwill

To AKa

K Dobrowolska

2018   x

"I don't know where I am going but I am on my way"

FRANCOIS-MARIE AROUET 'VOLTAIRE'

ISBN 978-1-78222-577-5

Book design, layout and production management by Into Print
www.intoprint.net
+44 (0)1604 832149

THE LETTER 'M'

Jenna knew she was born special and different from other people. She was gifted the letter M on both palms baring a skin scratched symbol of a driven woman, self-motivated, and artistic. She paints pictures free flowing and her art work is unique. Jenna has a clairsentience gift of deep empathy perception, and she feels emotions strongly. This shows through her unusual 'spirit' paintings. She teaches her style of art in tutorial evening classes and sells art work online. Jenna shares her home with her lazy sister Katrina and pet dog and cat. She prefers to live alone in isolation with her pets, but both parents died when Katrina was 15 years old and Jenna became Katrina's guardian. Katrina wasn't helpful in contributing to the household, and the food cupboard was bare. Jenna felt irritated and a crazy bubble head engulfed her tiredness. She felt depressed and low, attendances for art tuition were poor, and the effort to go to the shop to restock the food cupboard seemed a heavy burden in her mind.

"No milk. No bread. No washing powder." Jenna seethed. "I will have to go to the corner shops." Her moods start to fester, smothering her kind heart. She impulsively grabbed her handbag shouting

"Do you need anything from the shop Katrina?"

Katrina ignored her because she was wearing earphones and watching a movie on her phone. Kip barked hoping to be walked but Jenna shook her head. "Not this time cutie." She stroked Kips nose and hugged him. "You are a gorgeous pup. Love you."

Normal day. Normal shopping day. Normal routine. Normal life.

THINGS CHANGE

Jenna has become a spirit of euphoric 'astral body' energy, floating through the wind. The air colourfully shaded with blue and pink tinges, streaks of yellow, and orange glows. She sees her house from the corner of the road, her dog sitting on the sofa staring longingly out of the window. The air felt tight. Pressured. She felt incomplete, like a puppet on gluey strings. Jenna's 'spirit' powered her astral body and Jenna was naively surreal unaware of her circumstances.

Life is a disorganised mess. Frustration. Annoyance. Disbelief.

This is strange. Hazy waves of colour. Crazy life. Crazy living. Fast life and fast living. She is rejuvenated the speed is exhilarating.

Fast Movement. Fast air. Freedom. She feels energetically powerful.

Jenna enters her home through the open back door and saw Katrina cuddling her brown dog Kip. Tabby cat Chip lay purring on the rug.

"Kip, Jenna is not coming back … she's

never coming back." Katrina buried her distraught shocked face in Kip's smooth fur while stroking his ears at the same time. Kip nuzzled her face in sympathy. They sat on the sofa feeling lost.

Jenna couldn't see what the fuss was about. The air in the room was burdened with unhappiness.

"Sister is crying, Kip is whimpering, the air around them is stifling." Jenna didn't belong, she needed to escape and get out of the house. The atmosphere was intense, heavy and gloomy, and she couldn't understand why her sister felt low and tearful. Kip jumped off the sofa and ran around in circles. Chip sniffed the air, his whiskers twitching, then arched his back, and ran out of the back door.

The unsettled dog and cat could sense her presence so with a surge she propelled swiftly through the closed window to leave the house and didn't feel the glass as she manoeuvred through it. "Why haven't I bumped into the glass? I can see the glass in the window and can fly through it. Cool but weird and strangely satisfying."

Jenna wandered to the end of the road and as she turned the corner to the next street she saw a young man looking down, peering with a grim face. He was eyeing the ground and examining the bundle on the floor from all angles and contemplating his next action.

Lying on the gritted road was a broken body. Hair bloodied, legs bent, bulged eyes wide open. Hands bruised purple, fingers mangled, clothes torn apart, stomach deflated, and belly skin torn. Congealed blood and faeces splattered across the pavement and the neighbours' window pane. Gravity slowed Jenna drawing her to the person on the ground. Traffic curving round the scene. Routine normal for them. Life goes on. Sometimes it doesn't for some.

The man put on a pair of gloves and a mask to clear the mess.

Jenna moved closer. Attached to the body was a silver cord.

"OH NO!"

"Holy Shit! Lord please forgive my sins."

A sliver of a thin invisible silver cord was pulling at her spirit through the air and a glowing orb hovered around the cord becoming tighter, tighter, tighter, SEVERED!

"DEAD"

How can life change in a flash and be replaced by unexpected death? Hit and run biker your karma is under scrutiny because you didn't stop. You ran over her twice hoping she was killed outright but she clung on even though she was bleeding to death and defecating, and now she was slipping away and

ASCENDING

out of her body and letting her soul separate. Her silhouetted body spirit weightlessly lifted higher through the air relieved to leave behind a broken shell as part of her troubled past.

Has Jenna done enough in past life to end her suffered life with a fruitful happier afterlife? Will karma act gracious or will it be hellish?

Jenna felt the light fall dark behind her. She felt a presence and a lot of cold vibes. The air became warmer, illuminating, and then she saw the clan her

DECEASED FAMILY

in the shape of spiritual orbs. Luminous opaque spheres with blue rays transmitting vibes to absorb Jenna's spirit to their electrical energy encouraging her to follow them. Jenna wasn't ready to transfer over to the 'afterlife' so she raised her energy strength to embrace her family in a farewell stance and with a surge of electrical spirited power she transformed into a blue aura orb, then flung herself away from her orb family. Jenna's spirited strength and accumulated great power pirouetted her into the next level of transition and she became a soul orb. Distressed souls stay as astral bodies and were known as grounded ghosts because they couldn't transit to a higher spiritual realm. Jenna's soul changed into her family line intuitive blue aura orb, and she was determined to stay because she refused to enter the unknown afterlife.

Jenna's blue soul aura expanded larger and she moved away with a forceful speed leaving a mist of smoky blue haze lingering in the air. Jenna is led by the only thing that didn't break into pieces. Her soul. The soul stayed intact when her life caught short unexpectedly.

The accident happened on the way back from a trip to the local shop. She was lost in an oblivious high mental state of anxiety and didn't see the motor bike at full speed when she crossed the road. Anxiety happens quickly in mood disorder and the tragedy happened after buying food. Grey haze as she hit the ground with a thud. Death wasn't instant, the side of her body 'punched' on motor bike impact. Blood congealed blobs splattering the biker bonnet and mirror when her head hit the road.

Jenna was failing terminally.

Confused senses costing her life. Jenna didn't like life, that's why depression strangled her living. Living life is unkind.

People turned against each other and became violent. Land killings contributed to worldwide distress. Society was self-centred, selfish, careless and oblivious in thought, lacking skills in social communication, and forgetting how to enjoy life simply. People focused on the latest technology and gadgets available, and the expenditure for living was predominant in mind. No one realises that everything invented, inspired, prophesised, written, acted upon, leads to the same thing. *'Mind Evolution'* built from daily thought processed mind waves from everything living.

Mind waves create thought pattern changes. Mind waves create movement. Creative materialism. Creative thoughts. Create a journey. Mind waves are life changing for innovative modern way of living and a burden for controlling business and personal finances. The standard of living increased ludicrously high, and the health services diminished under corporate businesses owned by multi affluent figures in society. The environment suffered with severe climate changes from pollutions. Plants and animal species in abundance were becoming extinct.

Jenna is better off dead. Jenna is happier now she is dead. Death is surreal. The earth is known to be round but has become pear-shaped. Discriminating hatred in humanity, crushed the spirit in Jenna. The world is a dire place to live. People behave badly. Evil, destructive, materialistic, uncaring and selfish. Life has turned needy for the greedy.

Positive mind waves create positive things. Negative mind waves create disaster. Jenna was educated in world faith knowledge. She felt angered over ignorant people who blamed religions for the world turning haywire. Religions bore the brunt of people's failures, and humanity should really blame itself for ignorance, misjudgements, racial abuse, hatred and wars. Patriotism has become power mad. Bad world decisions. Bad Leaders in charge. Bad media output.

Misleading. Confusing. Unsettling. No security financially or emotionally.

Harsh world that is governed by greed, power, bribery, and discreet secret service killings. Chemical Companies created man-made poisons shamefully with no thought, and humanity was chained to conforming. Technology stalking everyone robbing personal information. Identification linked to a central computerized brain. People registered and recorded. Violation of privacy. Big Brother? no one needs a spy!

Jenna died through mind suffocation, crazed from world worry and unhappy living, and poisoned by breathing in the air of a hatred society of anarchists and vigilantes, and a loony biker who was high on throttle speed. He survived. Jenna died and survived too, by

SOUL POWER

That one moment in time killed her. The bread, butter, cheese, eggs milk, and washing powder were strewn across the other side of the street. No doubt the neighbours will pick up the best of what's left.

They cannot afford their weekly shopping. Living was harsh.

Jenna's sister Katrina heard the bike screech, then a loud thud, and no one could save Jenna. Only the body picker saw the last breath that made her shudder to death. Temporarily Jenna gained loose freedom to explore her surroundings, so her astral body rose with a trial awakening, and she visited her family home and saw her sister distressed but was unaware of her own personal circumstances.

The silver cord severed, released a celestial knowledge, she knew she was powering a blue intuitive soul aura and began to experience flash backs of her life. Her mother's scent lingered in the air and happy childhood days playing with friends in fields and upon hills. Teenage years of first love. Fighting with ex partners.

Jenna's previous life was challenging, and her soul danced to the tune of frenzied past emotions. Memories flipped with elevated speed and Jenna ascended higher pulling her towards the trees. Autumn is a pretty season. The leaves colourfully tinted in shades of yellow, red, brown and gold, falling softly into mounds of paisley flora. Energy surrounds all living things and trees produce oxygen and manufacture into functional materials. Oxygen and glucose molecules produce the fruit and tree sap is used in food and medication. Trees are important for earth's atmosphere and the gift for breathing in life. Jenna liked trees, she liked

THE PARK

a calming place to rest one's soul and a relaxed feeling amongst the bluetits and wagtail birds. It's wonderful to be so uninhibited, wild and free. Free from anxiety and a heavily burdened body. Jenna didn't miss her family or her friends as death doesn't accommodate grief, and only living people can grieve. Jenna's soul graciously uplifted. The knock from the motorbike woke her then killed her depression. She didn't know she was dying until she saw herself lying on the ground waiting to be cleared up like rubbish shoved in a skip lorry. Bad man biker. He should have asked if he wanted her dead. Careless thugs should be courteous not ruthless.

The deceased family line beckoned her to join them and she refused to leave the earth. Jenna was a stubborn woman. She wasn't going to succumb to death eternally, unless the eternal path led her to other spirited souls who were like her. Orange tree heaven would be great. She was dead and her

SOUL IS ALIVE

Jenna didn't cross over to the afterlife because she didn't know the best path to cross over. There were too many different beliefs of heaven and hell. During her life time she wanted people and the earth to revolve round her, and now it was her chance to hang on to her freed soul and cross over when she was ready. The force of her soul energy was vitalizing and enigmatic, and she flew to where she felt peace, a river a few miles away. Jenna was an earthbound soul orb and she was staying that way. For now. A free spirit in life deserves a free spirit in death. Jenna's eyes were beautifully soulful. The eyes died but the soul shot out of her

SPIRITUAL WINDOW

The Human eye is like a camera and witnesses life patterns. The soul absorbs life memories some are remembered and some lost. The human brain is the computer. Neuron cells transmit information and molecules orchestrate how people feel, act and react. The structures inside the brain are microtubules holding consciousness through quantum gravity, and this is the human diary of a person's existence. The soul consumes the inputs of the mind because the soul is pure energy of intensity and is immortal. The observant eye is

'THE WINDOW OF THE SOUL'

Jenna's soul performed a spiritual awakening after death when her eyes became lifeless after her body shattered. Jenna won't conform to the next stage of life because she wants answers. Where do you go to find peace after the last breath? Energy barriers surround everything living on earth. Earth is energy. Positive energy is well-being. Negative energy is destructively ill. Life is energy waves. Fauna, flora and humans output the energy waves whether they are useful or not creating functional living and this determines in a life time the outcomes of well-being, success, ill-health and tragedies.

Jenna is determined to keep her own decision and choice even in death. Her choice to finding everlasting life if it did exist. Some-how? Some-where? She has golden bravery stamped into her soul. She is a wild soul angel and fearless, and strong enough to tell the devil she would whip his tongue out and spit on the snake next to him.

A shadow cast over her. Her soul vibrated shivers. Someone was breathing on her was this God or was it the Devil? It was neither it was another grounded soul. She tried to connect with the shadow, a grey aura, but when she tuned in her blue energy towards the grey vibes, the grey aura clashed with hers and bounced back. Negativity energy clashes cut deep, an electromagnetism shock for both souls. The grey soul aura colour deepened a darker grey and ballooned to embrace her negative wounds. Jenna found it difficult to respond and the rejected soul flung itself over the river and disappeared into the distance. Wrong friendship Jenna thought. Wrong energy waves, wrong wavelength. Jenna's soul orb needed a similar energy twin.

Grey soul auras block energies, and cause conflict with other souls.

The river seemed lonely no human figure in sight, only an angry swan hissing at her and a bluish grey heron sat on the embankment proud and upright. The heron lifted himself and spanned out his wings, flying swiftly onto the roof top of a disused factory outlet.

The angry swan flapped his wings viciously sensing Jenna's soul, so Jenna flew forward alongside the river bank. She refused to fly over the river in case it was a crossing for the River Styx. The River Styx separates the world of the living from the world of the dead. The river is the border of consciousness, where there is no return for a soul when crossed over. Jenna wanted to avoid crossing over

THE RIVER STYX

because the River Styx is known as the river of hate and named after Styx the Goddess from the underworld in Greek Mythology. When the soul reaches the river Styx, a boatman named Charon would give a ride to the underworld ruled by Hades. The deceased would need to have a coin to pay Charon, and when the souls reached the other side they waited to be reborn, and life in the underworld was a consciousness frozen state of karma where you stayed as you died.

Jenna was a well-read woman and she was at the crossroads of her death. Careful consideration of afterlife journey was necessary. Jenna's soul felt comforted with water and air as she inherited a fiery birth sign and her personality was strong, passionate, and formidable. Now in death her soul was aligned with the calmness of water, but she didn't want to live her eternal life in the Hades underworld seas of wicked death. Jenna preferred to fly, and though she read that Greek hero Achilles was bathed in the River of Styx and gained immortality,

Jenna knew this pathway of eternity wasn't her immortality. Jenna's path was a journey of a higher realm of consciousness she wanted to ride with the clouds and beyond. The sky dimmed to a moody dark slate and the wind raised power, and her soul wave vibe orb flowed further along the river. She reached a

BRIDGE

and stopped, as a bridge can be a bridge of judgement in death. The Chinvat Bridge and the Bridge of As-Sirat are bridges of crossings into hell. Jenna flew under the bridge and met a man sat cross-legged with hands upturned in an umbrella greeting.

The man shut his eyes and hummed a sound hitting the bridge roof vibrating and echoing loudly. The water rippled slightly and water birds on either side of the bridge ruffled their feathers. The moor hens scurried to the other side of the embankment and the angry swan sailing down the river bank screeched and honked aggressively. The wise man looked around he could feel Jenna's presence.

"Come closer lost one let me feel your energy" he whispered gently.

Jenna hovered next to him and the dense feeling of knowing herself dead diminished. The tranquillity of the river and the man meditating gave her a sense of fulfilment. Anger dispels quickly if a soul places itself against a peaceful situation.

The man began to chant. He was middle-aged, his darkened skin had years of wisdom creases, his hair a raven coloured mop under a white Gandhi cap, and his eyes a humble brown. He wore old, holed, frayed clothes and open-toed sandals presenting an overall dishevelled appearance. He looked dedicated as if he was on a personal mission to change the world to something better. He opened a sandwich box and placed his lunch in front of him, an apple, satsuma, raisins, and cheese in flat bread. He lit a small candle with matches he kept in his pocket and holding the candle, he gently swayed it, and then proceeded to chant a prayer for Jenna's deceased soul. He was using his lunch as a food offering for her soul to find the path to eternity.

Jenna's soul quivered feeling the kindness and the prayers of the spiritual man. Jenna's aura shone a tinge of silver edging the blue colour.

The man was honouring Jenna's death which was normally reserved for family. The blue started to disperse and disappear. Silver streaks germinated and spread overcoming the blueness. The silver aura orb represented awakening of the cosmic mind. The wise man was trying to help

Jenna's soul orb grow more knowledgeable. People don't see auras and orbs unless they have special qualities that enable them to see. Jenna was gifted. Jenna could feel and see aura in her lifetime. Jenna's sixth sense will find the eternal place of peace. Empathy and intuition lives on in the soul, and

ETERNAL SOUL MISSION

has begun. The man stopped chanting and spoke wisely.

"Lost child, your sad existence will improve in the afterlife, your burdens will fade away and you will reincarnate when Brahma feels is fitting for you."

Jenna's energy started to fireball and her magnetic silver aura orb radiated a vivacious brightness as she flew through the bridge frenetically, silently thanking the praying man for his kind words. Jenna reached the other end of the bridge and realised she was still grounded, if she flew above it she would have crossed over with no turning back. Prayers from strangers along her soul journey are a blessing. She felt an ambience of tranquillity, and her effervescent silver spirited soul shimmered and glowed as she floated along the towpath. She liked the idea of reincarnation, and a dove would have suited her desires for peace and feeling free in flight. She flew into a dense suffocating area. The air was clear but felt like a sucked in vacuum, and this caused Jenna's soul to distort and flail erratically in all directions and she became out of control.

The area breathed violent deaths where extreme negativity of past evil events never moved souls on. The souls stayed naked in the atmosphere where evil reigned their life. Some souls re-incarnated with similar patterns of life if they didn't live morally, and some souls perished into structures and solid materials. No one is re-incarnated in the same life form. Karma decides the future of the deceased who were worthy or unworthy.

Jenna's soul was hovering over a haunting bleak place. The dense feeling air were sad souls suffocating themselves. Jenna's soul became paralysed and she lost the ability to move freely. The punished souls gripped her silver aura and they weren't going to let her go, and her soul waves looped circles dragging the pressured air strangulating her soul with distortion as the dark side of the afterlife embraced her, pulling her towards a charnel house.

The building held bones of evil past unearthed centuries ago when excavated for development, and a worship hall was standing behind a tree. In the distance two men walked along the river bank; a tall, bearded man with a blue turban and a Kirpan sword swinging below his tunic, and the other man was swathed in a white gown from head to foot, his mouth covered with a cloth. The two men sat down at a bench table near the river as they approached Jenna. They both shut their eyes in prayer, worship and meditation.

Jenna's soul hovered above them her suffocation relieved, and the thick soul air retreated to the charnel. Jenna's soul was saved by the turban praying wise protector and a peace abiding monk who didn't want her to be inflicted by other souls' bad karma. Jenna's soul must avoid hell on earth as soon as the air changed heavily. Hell is not in the sky or fire. There's no escape from earth's hell. Souls who bore unkindness as humans stayed on earth's hell until they could raise their energy to a higher pure plane, and evil souls were set in solid materials. Hell is air of burning smell, ash, and irritating gas. Satan asphyxiates the unworthy, slow suffocating death and distortion, and turmoiled confusion in Hell's eternity on the earth.

Heaven is only obtained by the energy of souls who spiritually lift themselves to the highest plain. Humans can start the process through various forms of enlightenment, such as meditation, yoga, reiki, holistic approaches and through individual and congregational unity of prayer and faith, also using empath abilities and psychic gifts to benefit their soul and others' well-being. To be aware of the seven chakras that flow as your energy through your body is important, because if they get blocked illness will manifest tenfold. Jenna was sure that her inner love for all things created, was returning kindness back to her along her soul journey, and spiritual living humans were helping to guide her soul orb safely, to help her reach her eternal destination she yearned to fulfil.

The golden rule of the Universe states, if you want to be treated kindly you should treat others kindly too. Jenna circled the two kind spiritual men and her aura breathed Namaste as she continued her path to find eternal happiness and the right moment to cross over.

She travelled to a pretty place she loved as a child. A Country Park.

Hills, a stream, trees, a small museum and café, and relics of an old castle. The Park was quiet only two dog walkers having a morning stroll, the dogs wagged their tail as Jenna's soul passed them. She came to a stream with a small waterfall and sat by the stream was a young man meditating. He was leaning against the tree cross legged and his hands touched together thumb to thumb and finger to finger, his head shaved. He wore loose robe clothing. Jenna felt her energy waves decreasing to slow motion. The man looked incredibly chilled. A pink aura generated around him and Jenna's lively soul became calm in the man's peaceful moment. The world has mismatched people cohabitating in abundance from bad mating decisions. Animals fared better at pairing up for life than humans, and Jenna wished she had inherited the calmness of the meditating man in her previous life, avoiding the difficult conflicts of relationships she endured unhappily until death. Her silver aura crackled as her soul bounced off the man's aura and she gained pink hue vein threads in the silver glow. The calm man didn't believe in a soul, he believed in existing and transferring energy to free himself of negativity hurt and ill-thought and achieve purity and oneness to raise mind waves to the highest peace possible. Would the world be interesting if everyone was totally calm? there wouldn't be a diversity of different people. Emotions shape individuals no one wants to be a clone of the same emotion. The man was kind and his gentle manner was humbly soothing. The pink aura around him radiated sensitivity, love and freedom, but Jenna liked her high-spirited aura, it needed toning down not stamped out. Time to go back to her

HOME

She returned to her house and received a light clash of an electric flash as she soared into her home road. God's time blip! Lightning electrical waves hit street lighting and the road blipped through a time tunnel. God controls time movements, not a clock. The trees sprouted much taller and the front door and outer cladding of the houses were renovated. Previously the houses in the street were red bricked and now coated with metal sheets. Jenna flew straight through the shut window, and the air pressure became intense and her soul manoeuvred a shapeless mass through weapon proof glass.

Jenna saw her sister Katrina sitting in a pod touch screening. Kip sat in a large lit cube old looking but still cute. The lights were healing for his aged bones, and Chip was immortalised in a digitally animated form. Pictures of Chip created a projection of his image to bounce off the wall into imaginary lifeform, and he looked real as he lay on the rug and then jumped on the sofa. Katrina couldn't bear to let go of Chip after losing Jenna, so immortalised him as a digital image ghost cat. Katrina wore a silver specked Jerkin and weapons were tucked inside the inner lining. Katrina's hair was a striking cobalt blue with a yellow Tuscan sun streak, and she bore clawed marks on her face. She looked fiercely formidable. Katrina's skin-tight dark grey leggings enhanced her toned legs and she wore high black frosted studded boots. Both hands were gun-metal banded with crystal spikes across the knuckles. The clawed face was the result of intruder invasion.

No one will target Katrina without bloodshed from her knuckle weapons. Katrina's pod contained sachets of energy food, hot and cold water, visual screen for viewing world news, visual screen for detecting neighbouring enemies, and a huge touch screen ready to activate and deactivate activities. The pod was metallic black with silver specks and the outer shell nuclear proof.

A mature crimson red-headed woman in silver shades entered the house, and Katrina left her pod putting on high resolution black shades to protect her eyes from the ultra violet lighting in the ceiling. She embraced her visitor. They touched each other's foreheads with two fingers and then palm touched each other's stomach. The woman wore a black Jerkin and grey marbled studded boots. She put her spiked gloved hand in the lining and retrieved energy food and speaking in a Slavic accent, she gave Katrina the sachets.

"Only one a day you are rationed. The Nihilist Scientist Presidency have withdrawn part of your food supply for not deactivating nonconformist memory patterns quick enough. You must work quicker if you miss one no more meals for you."

Katrina raised her voice in temper, her hands gripping her slim hips. She sternly eyeballed her senior leader and flicked her long dark wavy hair in annoyance, and angrily she blurted

"I am tired of living in the pod Janika. I search for people's identities, check on anarchist activities, mind bust enemies, and explore the world from home. It's a prison. I might as well be with Jenna."

Katrina was head worn. She was claustrophobic under the new regime order. The Nihilist Presidency Scientists were fighting for a new world. Millions of Nihilist supporters worldwide wanted to eradicate the minority of maniacal terrorists who killed innocent people. The Nihilist Presidency were getting stronger and overthrowing the Government body of the world's countries, so they could endorse new policies and create an equal world for all ethnic cultures to conform to, enabling a peaceful existence without exercising their personal belief. Families imprisoned within homes was an extreme curfew but until all the imposing enemy were mind cleared the law was indefinite. Freedom of living would be reinstated when purity of same thought pattern was in everyone's

MIND

Jenna's soul started to waver grey patches. Sadness. Human rights were sanctioned. The air span between her and her sister was wide apart, she was viewing her sister through a future era. Katrina had aged by 15 years. 150 years forward through quantum time blip. Kip, old and frail was held in a cube for his well-being. Memories of Chip were flashing on the wall and Chip looked eerily spectral. Janika was Katrina's employer, her mentor and guide. Jenna felt misplaced, as home was a hi-tech fortress. Home wasn't the home she remembered. Katrina was a freedom fighting warrior not her sister.

The Nihilist Presidency office would reinstate freedom of speech when they were sure that every person was mind-cleansed. *Voltaire, Albert Einstein* and *Baruch Spinoza* hung as digital portrait Icons in the Presidential Palace. The Junior Academy of future Nihilist Scientists laser beamed the portraits from a diamond chip in the palm of their hand to hear digital voices of historical facts, and learn from the two philosophers and the theoretical physicist who inspired revolutionary changes in the eras they were born in. The Nihilist Scientists believed future scientific discoveries would greatly improve without the conflicts of faith, culture, and moral and immoral decisions contributing to madness and atrocities of war. Cloning a 'same thought patterned' world without religious intolerance was imminent. The Nihilist Scientists are celestial time travellers evolved from the Star Seed children.

Katrina's home was renovated for war zone. She was awarded ultra violet lighting to sterilise her air from pollutions because she chose to freedom fight in isolation. Cultural Anarchism reached a peak when Jenna's soul time-warped into the future. Katrina was head worn from touch screening mindwiping buttons daily. The routine was tedious, isolated and unethical, and Katrina's mind was radicalised and exhausted from performing the tasks required.

Written on the door leading to a botanical conservatory attached to the house stated:

"Cultural Anarchism is important – indeed essential – because authoritarian values are embedded in a total system of domination with many aspects besides the political and economic."

Secular education was executed. Faith preaching banned. Freedom of speech in public censored, and media coverage vetted and restricted. Life was lonely living in a

POD

Families worldwide owned a pod. All families were given a choice, to fight to keep their cultural faith and allegiance to worship, or to put faith into the Nihilist Presidency Scientists and become a world without religious belief. The Nihilist Presidency Scientists believed that God is a supreme entity energy force of light, and upon death a person joins to the supreme light eternally. People are born into a cycle of life, death, and the last breath blows into pure energy resting in the air and light, and the and life can only be re-energised again by evolving new mutating cells. There is only existence, survival, and death whatever form it breeds. Energy is the power that causes something to exist and move, and energy is born through God's electrical light and chemical formations infusing within developing life forms, evolving wherever they settle in the earth and water, and procreate. Human beings do not come back into existence in the same life pattern.

The war is between

RELIGION and SCIENCE

No life outside the pod. Every living thing outside homes would eventually die through lack of care, because it was more important to overthrow people imposing their beliefs on others. Freedom of speech was acceptable with mentor but not exercised elsewhere.

The Courts of Justice who previously governed criminals to trial had crumbled in the rebel uprising. The Nihilists Scientists built an external conservatory for every home who conformed to the new system enabling families to breathe in medical flora and aid sanity. Children were self-educating themselves within educational pods at home. People chosen as mentors, health workers, maintenance workers, and emergency service workers left their pods to work externally when needed, but these were few in numbers. Only one super skilled technician per area performed the task of many. Conventional medicines had ceased too, and natural remedies were reinvented because plant life was growing wild in abundance without farming and gardening maintenance. Medical workers reaped in the plants to produce natural medicines and the mentors distributed 'healing flora medicine' to the homes who served 'The Nihilist Presidency' with most loyalty. Medical health care and government buildings were deserted so

COMMUNAL PRODUCTIVITY

ceased to exist. Buildings used as commercial businesses, retail parks, hospital and retail hypermarkets became a sanctuary to house the masses of homeless unemployed, and those who were dysfunctional and ill. People suffered risk of death through pollutions in the air and lacked food and water. They were abandoned because of weak minds and poor lifestyle. Zoos closed, and the wild animal kingdom freed and left to forage and roam naturally. Domesticated animals were cubed for their safety or destroyed. Smaller food stores became depleted through the vigilantes pilfering, destroying shops and factories. Energy sport food supplements developed more concentrated to accommodate less food needs in hindsight of the scale of the cultural wars. People conditioned themselves to living off two energy formula or dehydrated sachets a day, and travel was grounded indefinitely.

Everyone was trapped in the towns and cities they inhabited, and suicide was happening on a massive scale. People were drained mentally, and madness multiplied, and the mental health support receded, through lack of educated support workers.

When Jenna was alive living was becoming sterile. Dead bodies were picked up and disposed of quickly. Memorial stones were bulldozed in favour of small peace gardens and the stones recycled for other purposes. The deceased ashes scattered amongst the flowers with no memorials to distinguish families. Families against cremation were buried in natural burial grounds unidentified and generated a healthy income for landowners.

Katrina didn't see Jenna's body. She was informed by the security forces. People information of identity developed through the eyes, and the body picker intercepted Jenna's dying eyes before her soul severed and relayed her DNA and personal information to the security central information bank. The security forces informed Katrina that Jenna was dead by transmitting the information to her media viewing screen. Seeing a deceased family member was banned and grieving discouraged.

Now in the future era 150 years forward, people didn't verbally speak unless they were asked a question. Disciplined discretion and silence was compulsory. The Nihilist Presidency Scientists are super intelligent powered celestial beings formed out of energy and developed to look like intelligent scientifically minded humans, with a goal to create a peaceful united thought process for all.

Jenna quantum leaped her soul through an earth bounded twin paradox and she saw the future controlled by celestial humans. The alien scientist humans watched the earth destroying itself by conflicts of humans' emotional errors and landed on the earth to cleanse the minds of people, to become one race.

There was nothing Jenna could do for Katrina or Kip, Janika was Katrina's family. Jenna was in soul transition and needed to complete her mission of discovering the eternal path and with a great force of energy power Jenna flew through the bullet proof window, and stepped back through the gateway of her previous era to explore the

HOLY SACRED BUILDINGS

Jenna flew to visit three worship buildings and her soul was greying in sadness because the religious cultural traditions would not be reinstated in the Nihilist uprising. Religion and heritage were important for the history and ancestry of people's descendants. Jenna needed to explore the holy buildings to feel the environment. Who wants to be imprisoned like her sister Katrina? forced to analyse personal information and input destruction in human minds in a man-made shell of a home. Jenna was glad she was dead. She had dropped out of a mortal life when it was still real to her and at least freedom of living and the choice of enjoying life was still there. Jenna decided to power fly into a

CITY

Jenna flew towards a worship building with a history of antisemitism persecutions. Jenna's soul entered a beautifully crafted building with wooden and golden coloured interiors. Cheerful Hanukkah candles flickered glowing warmth in the building. Holiness shone in the atmosphere.

The worship hall bestowed an atmospherically spiritual wellbeing.

The religious community of people believed in going to a special place in the afterlife to await to be re-joined as one faith again to reclaim the land they lost in persecution. This community of people were humble and hard-working and performed moral duties and acts of worship to gain rewards after death. Jenna sensed this place of worship was a closed community, it was sacred and very restricted. Jenna's soul felt misplaced, she was shining an aura of grey with specks of pink and silver, and now her soul was gaining illuminous yellow streaks, which dispersed the mangled colours creating a sunshine warmer glow. Jenna was gaining spiritual awareness of hope and optimism and the building atmosphere was trying to absorb her interest. Jenna had always viewed life open minded and free spirited and everyone's beliefs were important for the growth of humanity and evolution. The Hanukkah candle lamps were the focal object Jenna's soul was drawn to, and her aura felt the dedication of the people and their faith to God. Jenna was thankful for gaining hotter aura from the lamps shine and she left the building with a clearer vision of a soul mission as she shone warm exhilarating heat, beaming a yellow Incandescent gleaming charismatic soul aura.

Jenna moved forward to the next building to soul search

DRACONIAN or TRUTH?

Further into the City Jenna saw a beautiful dome-shaped building, men draped in white robes with holy scripture literature tucked under their arm ready for prayers. Young boys dressed similar in white skull caps walking with their father to the building.

Jenna's soul aura started to shake, the feelings of these people were mixed. There was a peaceful side of nurturing and abiding by moral laws and actions, but there was also a very narrow-minded view of not accepting other faith belief. Mind empowerment and overpowering repetitive conditioning of the mind and actions to conform, creates a one road trip of ignorance. To mind stir belief in such a regime way can instigate madness and misinterpretations of what is learnt and how to live by it. Religious narcissism is a destructive force within all cultures and faiths of people. Humanitarian care in all ethnic and religious communities does unite in abundance when tragedies occur, but the Nihilists believed the human bonding would get stronger with equal mind thoughts. Jenna's soul felt heavy her aura suddenly turning dark ebony and colder, masking the warmth of the illuminous yellow. The soul was transforming because she was being drawn into a divine guidance of great strength and she realised her soul was clashing with the building, she was sensing a strong conformist atmosphere.

Worldwide anger festered because of a minority of cruel people who didn't accept anyone outside their faith, and targeted people with intimidating judgement and ignorance. Tensions were building, faith and trust diminished, and humanity increasing bitterness rapidly. Jenna's soul couldn't enter the building, as the wall of solidarity was strong and defensive, and her soul would have torn with not belonging inside. Jenna silently grieved "Everyone is the same. Why is this world of people going berserk? We all head the same way in soul crossing."

We all aim to be united with God. The bodiless soul can get depressed too. Jenna's soul grew heavier, she loved all people no matter where they came from. In death all people unite with God. Killing is an unnecessary action of great sin. Sacrilege, unethical, and contradicts the sanctity of life.

Jenna's soul ballooned a mass aura of a depressive darkness, she couldn't stop it from happening, and her moody ebony coloured soul began contracting in coldness when she fluctuated inconsistent rhythms through the air. Divine guidance was pushing her away from the building and she felt soul confusion. Jenna's energetic darkened soul expanded and with all the molecule air power she could muster, she forced herself away from the building. She began to understand why the Nihilist Presidency Scientist evolved. Hypocritical back-stabbing with a conditioned closed mind born bad change. Messy head war. Jenna fell out of it at the right time. Her eternal vision was becoming clearer and she realised her faith was in

JESUS

He did say he would come again to lead the worthy to eternal life? Jesus is the Light of the World.

Jenna was born into loving Jesus and Mother Mary with a strict disciplined life of prayers and church attendance, but her views changed as she matured. Jenna hovered in front of a small worship building on top of a hill. A statue of Jesus was embedded in the arch of the building holding his arms out to embrace her and welcome her home. The building emitted incense. The oppressive praying in repent lingered in the air. Jesus beckoned her to join him and Jenna succumbed in

PRAYER

"Lord Jesus, I need to decide when to cross over. I was living a turmoiled hell of unhappiness when I lived a human life and hell is still chasing me now I am dead. I wanted to save people's souls, yet my tongue has burnt fire to all around me. I could see in my body life people who acted against me. I received little praise in my lifetime and madness of minds is rife. I don't know what to do? am I worthy of any direction?"

Jenna's soul aura started to swirl around the statue of Jesus. Her soul heard the words: "The earth will be re-born" was this

THE SECOND COMING?

The earth was vulnerable. Killings increased daily. The mind war evolved into an independent individual person war on humanity. People are afraid to die alone and are misguided by their vision of eternal life. Destructive people seek ultimate idolatry glory in the afterlife. Buildings, transport, social venues, and technology built by people's increasing intelligence, violated and destroyed by continuous land wars. Madness worldwide triggered a chain of steps in global communication confusion.

Jenna's soul searched for peace in eternity, and at the same time people all over the world were living a nightmare. People were disease-crazed in their depressed brains causing self-destruction. People's minds all over the world were viral crazy and obliviously brain jumbled, by mass hysteria panicking, and fake information by the media. Living life was unsafe to enjoy for fear of a stranger attack spontaneously. Jenna's soul was severely turmoiled, and her unsettled desires to reach ultimate eternity fulfilment was turning her soul deathly black and gloomy. Jenna heard a familiar distant

VOICE

Katrina shouting erratically with fearful venom!

"We are flooding! We are flooding! The water is rising with wrath! Water has erupted everywhere, in every canal, river, lake, sea, ocean on earth. The Apocalypse has dawned all over the world!"

Jenna's soul swirled larger and larger she saw Jesus's eyes, the statue was changing and becoming a vision. Jesus had brown eyes, he had darker skin, dark hair, and Jenna's soul became confused. She started to dance air waves and the winds whipped up a howling gust. The trees blew with a force gale, leaves fell off in abundance causing a harlequin leaf storm. The sky doleful and sombre, the atmospheric air terminally brewing ferociously. Jenna's soul became frenetic, memories of Jesus with lighter hair, lighter skin, blue eyes, stirred her soul angrily. Jenna's soul was deceived by fake statue idols. Hearing Katrina's cries and seeing Jesus portrayed differently, kick-started her soul aura into a hurling tornado. The icons of this spiritual building were misleading. Jesus was physically portrayed differently when she alive. Jesus was a good man. Jesus was still in Jenna's soul in death. Jesus's teachings are truth. Jesus is the light of the world. The world became dark from people's selfishness, greed, discrimination, and corruptive behaviour. Jesus is loved by all.

Jenna's soul aura fermented into a confused turbulence. She could hear Katrina's frantic distressed warning and feel her pressing her touchscreen uncontrollably to warn people as water was beating against the house. God had promised that the flood would not appear again, but a promise only lasts the lifetime it was set in. The promise was broken. Is God to blame? Is God as bad as people?

NO!

No! No! No! people are the cause of their own destruction.

Now people are damned in the Apocalypse before them.

The earth flooding, lands caving in, creating phenomenal disasters.

Katrina's voiced echoed in Jenna's volatile gust of swirling soul.

'We have a storm a violent storm, the heavens have opened the lightning is flashing in all corners of the world. The lightning is striking every river, every sea, every ocean, making the water rise with fire in the waters. The world is in simultaneous

CHAOS!

People screaming, wailing, scared, praying. Buildings broken, windows smashed. Tornados, earthquakes, hurricanes violently stirring, whipping the airwaves in forceful destruction.

Technology was fast and powerful and now weak and crumbling. Pods fail in a large-scale natural disaster. Technology systems shutting down in a destructive worldwide domino effect.

The flooding and earthquakes causing masses of land parting. The dormant volcanos erupting with power and poison spilling out.

Animal life bolting, stampeding; man and beast cornered by Satan's earth fury.

Jenna's blackening tornado soul started to rise and balloon a much larger orb of energy. Her soul aura colour still mingled deposits of blue, silver, pink and yellow warmth, and the combination of warmth and coldness caused an extreme electrical current to circulate her orb, as she violated the sky. Lightning struck the Jesus worship building, bouncing off Jenna's electrified huge soul orb. Intense pressure, *FLASH!*

Jenna's soul blasted a plasma of bright light, that shot an explosion of electrical lightning light high into the universe and showering down into an amazing

NEON GLOWING ATOMIC RAIN-STORM

of coloured atom molecules, neurons, and cosmic dust. The light rays beamed downed to the earth's ground, and back up to the sky and beyond.

Jenna's soul electrically struck all soul auras on the earth and on higher planes, creating a new eternal path for a

NEW EARTH EXISTENCE

Souls have awoken in a new light. Previous bodied life forms all electrically terminated. Trees and plant life burned and frazzled by out of control fires. Buildings crumbled and destroyed. The earth has evolved as a planet of extreme circulating electrical energy and light.

SPINOZA

God is the highest pure energy harmonising all energies that exist.

The living forms of the future will evolve from positive and negative energies. Kind light and evil darkness will give birth to new energy life beings who will become strong and powerful. Jenna's soul aura didn't cross over. Her soul imploded and self-combusted.

She became a minutiae atom floating aimlessly through the Universe. Time is infinite. Air is timeless. Soul mission completed. Jenna did more than cross over to the afterlife, she created a new way of existence for other souls to join her.

GOD AND UNIVERSE ARE ONE
AND THE SAME

Kate Goodwill

*"All mortals are equal; it is not their birth
But virtue itself that makes the difference"*
VOLTAIRE

*"I believe in God who reveals himself in the
orderly harmony of the Universe"*
ALBERT EINSTEIN

*"The mind of God is ALL the mentality, that
is scattered over space and time, the diffused
consciousness that animates the world."*
BARUCH SPINOZA

*"As within, so without. What we expect, we
receive.
What we give out, we get back. What we
believe, becomes
our reality. Alignment and synchronicity,
with our soul calling
ultimately determines our happiness in life."*
TONY DIMMOCK
(Intuitive Empath & Coach)

"We are living as a human shell. Our bodies have internal astral bodies. Those that are aware they are sixth sense gifted, can hear their inner voices speak, and feel their inner actions move. The greatest Power is internal power. The greatest Voice is the voice of a united understanding, and the greatest Mind will be the mind of all who feel love, peace, joy and faith within themselves.

We are born to the Planet for a purpose of evolving our soul through light, healing, love and peace, and for the soul of our Earth."

Kate Goodwill

Lightning Source UK Ltd.
Milton Keynes UK
UKHW020245171019
351716UK00007B/1470/P